The Sea Otter

Mrs. Vizithum

Written by Maggie Blake

Tap, tap, tap, tap.
A sea otter lies on her back in the water,
preparing her lunch.
She holds a mussel in her mitten-like paws
and batters it against a stone balanced
on her chest.
Tap, tap, tap, tap.
It can take thirty or more blows
to break open the shell.
In between bites of shellfish,
she rolls over in the water
to wash her fur clean.

Francois Gohier

Many years ago,
sea otters learned to stay safely
at sea where food is plentiful.
But even at sea, they were hunted
by men who wanted to make
coats from the otters' long fur.
Now sea otters are protected.
They leave the sea only
when they are sick or old
and waiting to die.

Sea otters prefer to spend their days afloat on their backs, close to rocks and kelp beds, ready to disappear underwater in a flash if there are signs of danger.

Francois Gohier

But sea otters still have to be wary of people.
Some fishermen would like to kill them
for raiding the shellfish beds.
The otters have other enemies
to be wary of, too.
Sea otters have to watch for sharks,
and for eagles,
which dive through the air
and carry off their pups.

Enemies of the sea otter

Eagle

Great white shark

The sea otter's pup sleeps,
floating on a tangle of seaweed
in the rolling sea.
The pup was born in the water.
After the birth, it lay on its mother's
chest looking wonderingly at its watery home.
It was able to float by itself in the salty water
as soon as the mother sea otter had groomed
and fluffed its waterproof coat.

While the pup sleeps,
the sea otter dives for more food.
She keeps her stone with her,
tucked in a furry pocket on her chest.
When she has eaten, the sleek brown otter
lets the pup lie on her chest
sucking her warm, rich milk.
She sculls her powerful, furry tail
through the water, keeping them
both afloat.

A sleeping pup.

Later, the sea otter spends a whole hour
grooming her pup — squeezing water
out of its coat and blowing air into its fur.
She does the same to her own fur.
They both need to be groomed often
to keep their coats waterproof.
If their coats become waterlogged,
the sea otters get cold and die.

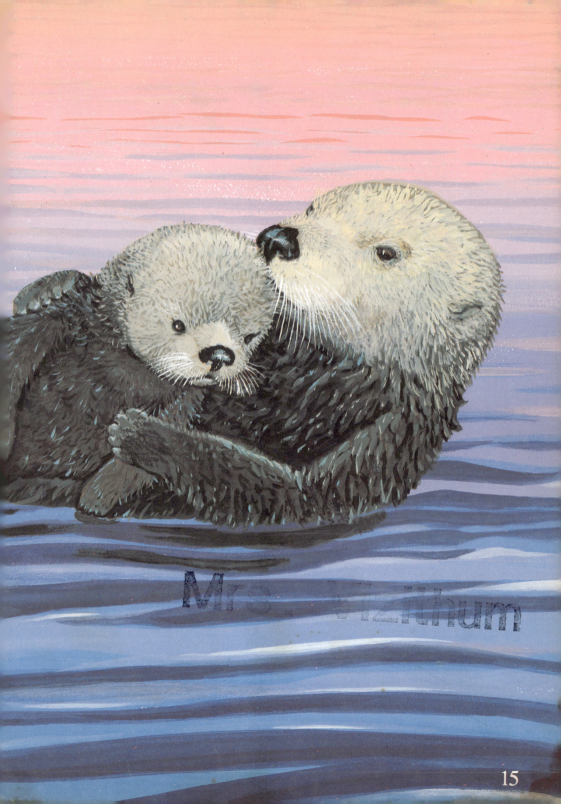

As the otter pup grows, it learns to dive among the long swaying stalks of kelp in its underwater playground.
There it is safe from eagles.
It enjoys playing hide and seek with other pups.

The pup never gets to meet its father. Mother and father otters get together for only a few days, while they mate. The father then goes back to live with a group of males.

François Gohier

The females band together, too.
They chortle, grunt, and whine
as they lie on their backs,
grooming their fur and feeding.
Sometimes there are as many as 200 of them
in a group.

Sea otters swim fast and can dive deep for up to a minute in search of food. Their favorite food is shellfish — clams, mussels, abalones.
They eat sea urchins, crabs, anemones, and any slow moving fish that passes by.

Favorite food of sea otters

Clam

Sea urchin

Mussel

Crab

Abalone

Sea anemone

An otter digs for clams with her forepaws. She uses a stone to pry abalones off the rocks, diving six or seven times after one abalone.

Diving for abalones.

When the water is murky,
the sea otter relies on a thick sprout of whiskers
around her muzzle to let her know
what is going on.
Through her sensitive whiskers, she can detect
the flash of a fish's tail.

A sea otter can unsheathe her claws like a cat to catch a fish. She then carries it to the surface and kills it with a bite close to its head. She tears off chunks of raw fish flesh and eats it.

A sea otter eating a white sea bass.

Another otter meal is octopus.
Its arms and suckers may grip the otter's
face, legs and even the inside of her mouth.
But she is not bothered at all.
Small octopuses often creep
into empty soft drink cans
lying at the bottom of the sea.
But that doesn't keep them safe from otters,
who have learned to reach the baby octopuses
by tearing open the cans with their teeth.

Fishing for food keeps an otter very busy.
But there is always time to rest.
Then the sea otter wraps some strands
of seaweed around her body to keep herself
from floating away.
With the sea gently rocking her,
she is soon fast asleep on her back.

Richard A Bucich

Fast asleep under a blanket of seaweed.

Index

birth	10
claws	26
enemies	4, 8
favorite foods	21, 28
finding and eating food	2, 4, 13, 20, 22, 26, 28
grooming	10, 14, 19
how sea otters use seaweed	10, 16, 30
hunting of sea otters	4, 8
living in groups	18-19
protection of sea otters	4
sea otter pups	8, 10, 13, 14, 16
using stones as tools	2, 13, 22
using tails	13
where sea otters live	6, Inside Back Cover
whiskers	25